America
My Country

editor
Maryjane Hooper Tonn

•

managing editor
John H. Hafemeister

O beautiful for spacious skies,
For amber waves of grain,
For purple mountain majesties
Above the fruited plain.
America! America!
God shed His grace on thee,
And crown thy good with brotherhood
From sea to shining sea.

Katharine Lee Bates

I pledge allegiance to my Flag and (to) the Republic for which it stands — one Nation indivisible — with liberty and justice for all,

Francis Bellamy

I pledge allegiance to the flag
of the United States of America
and to the republic for which
it stands, one nation, under God,
indivisible, with liberty and justice
for all.

This is the original Pledge of Allegiance to the flag in the handwriting of the author, Francis Bellamy, written at the decree of President Benjamin Harrison in 1892 to commemorate the 400th anniversary of the discovery of America. The original words have been changed on Flag Day in 1954 by an Act of Congress.

My Country

Reginald Holmes

It means the vast mountains that tower so high
To kiss the white clouds that float in the sky;
The deep surging ocean, the white sandy shore,
The crags and the boulders where wild breakers roar;
A cool shady forest and level green plains,
A herd of sleek cattle and old country lanes;
The fragrance of orchards when apple trees bloom,
The goldenrod's glint and the sumac's red plume . . .

A girl on a hilltop with wind in her hair,
The scent of the pine trees when April is there;
A cool mossy bank by a whispering stream
That flows through a meadow where buttercups gleam;
It means the great cities, the gay teeming throngs,
The men who make laws and the men who write songs,
The deep-canyoned streets where tall buildings instill
Our tribute to man's architectural skill . . .

The mills and the shops where the workingman's zeal
Gives birth to a thousand things fashioned of steel;
The tall-steepled churches where often is heard
The hymns of the faithful, the truth of God's word;
The homes and the schools that instruct and inspire
Our youth for the deeds their tomorrows require;
A land where the wanderer finds shelter and rest . . .
America, the home of the free and the blest!

©

I Love This Land

Evelyn Tooley Hunt

I love this land . . . from water's edge
To salt-gray marsh and the grass between,
With sea and sand and itinerant breezes;
The cormorant perched on his rocky ledge,
And the great bald eagle patrolling the sedge
Where the last late fish hawk may be seen.

I love this land . . . the frozen field
Where snow has quilted the sleeping earth,
But the murmur of melting never ceases.
Here, after winter begins to yield,
A garland of promise will be revealed
In hedgerows marking the meadow's girth.

I love this land . . . the golden plain
Where science and sinew together keep
The dream alive, as earth releases
Its reservoirs of yesterday's rain
To farmers planting perennial grain;
And the seeds of tomorrow are rooted deep.

I love this land . . . whose purple hills
Rise above vineyards heavy with sun,
Where finches strut on wire trapezes
And sing to yellow daffodils,
While spring's reluctant bounty fills
The crates of summer, one by one.

I love this land . . . where pioneers
Pursued success through bolts and bars,
And faith's investment still increases
In ever-widening frontiers,
As men walk Godward through the years,
Whose sky is bright with eternal stars.

Fourth of July Celebrations

Betty W Stoffel

Let there be prayers as well as great parades,
Let hymns combine with patriotic songs,
Let there be leaders of the future days,
With heroes of the past amid the throngs.
Let reverent silence punctuate the noise,
Let God be praised for this great land of ours,
Let sober meditation balance joys
And grave humility mark crucial hours.

Let statesmanship grow from this nation's need,
Let citizenship be equal to these days,
That godly men who gave their lives indeed
Be not betrayed by dull, indifferent ways.
Let joyfulness, not wildness, mark the free,
That God may find us worth our liberty!

From MOMENTS OF ETERNITY by
Betty W. Stoffel. Published by John Knox Press.
Copyright 1954. Reprinted by permission

A New World

Alice Crowell Hoffman

Columbus found a new world
Because he dared to do
A thing that was unheard of . . .
A thing that was quite new.

Columbus found a new world
Because he made a start,
Instead of merely pondering on
The thoughts within his heart.

Columbus found a new world
Because he saw things through.
And you can find your new world
Precisely that way, too.

Hold On To America

JoAnn M. Stiff

When Columbus discovered America,
He did not know that he had found
A land to be populated with free men,
Where peace and justice would abound.
A seed of truth was planted in the new land
That Columbus could not have known
Would be cultivated and nurtured in love
After it was carefully sown.

Men like Washington, Jefferson and Lincoln
Helped the seedling grow straight and tall.
And patriotic men have given their lives
So our nation would never fall.

May we always cherish this precious freedom,
Keep it tightly within our clasp.
There is no other government in the world
With such liberty in its grasp.
But to remain free we must do our duty,
Stand firm and staunch and pray;
God has given us a country richly blessed . . .
Let us help to keep it that way.

©

Give me your tired, your poor, your huddled masses, yearning to be free. The wretched refuse of your teeming shore, send these; the homeless, tempest-tossed to me. I lift the lamp beside the golden door.

Psalm 127:1

XCEPT
the LORD
Build
the house, they labour
in vain that build it.

PAUL
MANN

True Greatness

C. E. Flynn

A man is as great as the dreams he dreams,
As great as the love he bears,
As great as the values he redeems,
And the happiness he shares.

A man is as great as the thoughts he thinks,
As the worth he has attained,
As the fountains at which his spirit drinks,
And the insight he has gained.

A man is as great as the truth he speaks,
As great as the help he gives,
As great as the destiny he seeks,
As great as the life he lives.

©

Give Us Men

Mamie Ozburn Odum

Give us men to teach our children,
Men of courage and of scope,
Men that know eternal rightness,
Men of honor and of hope.

Give us men steady as mountains,
Men broad-minded as the plains;
Give us men with rightful living,
With high purpose in their mien.

Give us men for future leaders,
Men to meet life's stormy blast,
Men that have no fear in daring
As forefathers of the past.

Give us men to lead our nation,
Men that merge the heart and brain;
Men who stand up under pressure
When things go against the grain.

Give us men to lead us upward,
Men who are worthy of the sod,
Men to teach the rule that's golden,
Men who walk in fear of God.

Give us men of noble vision,
Standing strong in health and sorrow,
Building firm and ever upward
Ideals for a great tomorrow.

©

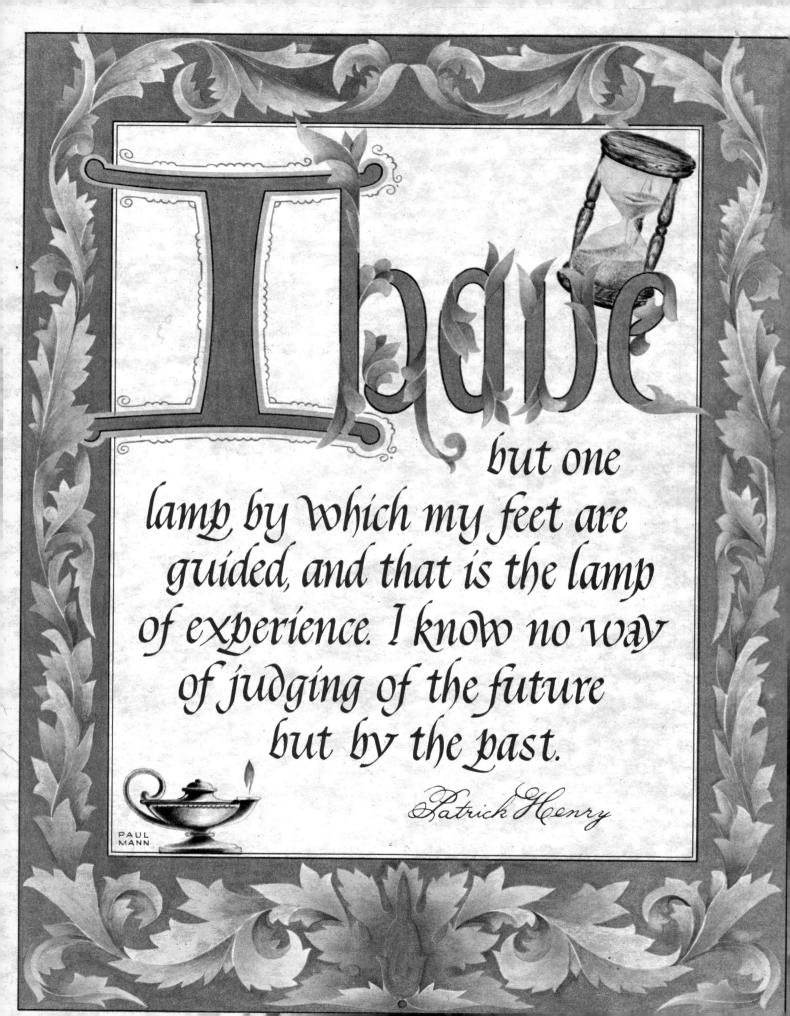

I have but one lamp by which my feet are guided, and that is the lamp of experience. I know no way of judging of the future but by the past.

Patrick Henry

PAUL MANN

The Coming American

Sam W. Foss

Bring me men to match my mountains,
  Bring me men to match my plains;
Men with empires in their purpose,
  And new eras in their brains.
Bring me men to match my prairies,
  Men to match my inland seas;
Men whose thoughts shall prove a highway
  Up to ample destinies;
Pioneers to clear thought's marshlands
  And to cleanse old error's fen;
Bring me men to match my mountains —
  Bring me men.

Bring me men to match my forests,
  Strong to fight the storm and blast,
Branching toward the skyey future
  Rooted in the fertile past;
Bring me men to match my valleys,
  Tolerant of sun and snow,
Men out of whose fruitful purpose
  Time's consummate blooms shall grow;
Men to tame the tigerish instincts
  Of the lair, the cave, and den,
Cleanse the dragon, slime of nature —
  Bring me men.

Bring me men to match my rivers,
  Continent cleavers, flowing free;
Drawn by the eternal gladness
  To be mingled with the sea;
Men of oceanic impulse,
  Men whose moral currents sweep
Toward the wide-infolding ocean
  Of the undiscovered deep;
Men who feel the strong pulsation
  Of the central sea, and then
Time their current to its earth throb —
  Bring me men.

*From WHIFFS FROM WILD MEADOWS by
Sam Walter Foss. Reprinted by
permission of Lothrop, Lee & Shepard Co.*

America, the Beautiful

Katharine Lee Bates

O beautiful for spacious skies,
For amber waves of grain,
For purple mountain majesties
Above the fruited plain.
America! America!
God shed His grace on thee,
And crown thy good with brotherhood
From sea to shining sea.

O beautiful for pilgrim feet,
Whose stern, impassioned stress
A thoroughfare for freedom beat
Across the wilderness.
America! America!
God mend thine every flaw,
Confirm thy soul in self-control,
Thy liberty in law.

O beautiful for patriot dream
That sees beyond the years,
Thine alabaster cities gleam,
Undimmed by human tears.
America! America!
God shed His grace on thee,
And crown thy good with brotherhood
From sea to shining sea.

America

Samuel F. Smith

My country, 'tis of thee,
Sweet land of liberty,
Of thee I sing;
Land where my fathers died,
Land of the Pilgrims' pride,
From ev'ry mountainside
Let freedom ring.

My native country, thee,
Land of the noble free,
Thy name I love;
I love thy rocks and rills,
Thy woods and templed hills;
My heart with rapture thrills
Like that above.

Let music swell the breeze,
And ring from all the trees
Sweet freedom's song;
Let mortal tongues awake;
Let all that breathe partake;
Let rocks their silence break,
The sound prolong.

Our fathers' God to Thee,
Author of liberty,
To Thee we sing;
Long may our land be bright
With freedom's holy light;
Protect us by Thy might,
Great God, our King.

SWORN UPON
WE HOLD THESE TRUTHS TO BE SELF-
EVIDENT: THAT ALL MEN ARE CREATED
EQUAL, THAT THEY ARE ENDOWED BY THEIR
CREATOR WITH CERTAIN INALIENABLE
RIGHTS, AMONG THESE ARE LIFE, LIBERTY
ND THE PURSUIT OF HAPPINESS, THAT
O SECURE THESE RIGHTS GOVERNMENTS
ARE INSTITUTED AMONG MEN. WE…
SOLEMNLY PUBLISH AND DECLARE, THAT
THESE COLONIES ARE AND OF RIGHT
OUGHT TO BE FREE AND INDEPENDENT
STATES…AND FOR THE SUPPORT OF THIS
DECLARATION, WITH A FIRM RELIANCE
ON THE PROTECTION OF DIVINE
PROVIDENCE, WE MUTUALLY PLEDGE
OUR LIVES, OUR FORTUNES AND OUR
SACRED HONOUR.

A Nation's Strength

Ralph Waldo Emerson

What makes a nation's pillars high
  And its foundations strong?
What makes it mighty to defy
  The foes that round it throng?

It is not gold. Its kingdoms grand
  Go down in battle shock;
Its shafts are laid on sinking sand,
  Not on abiding rock.

Is it the sword? Ask the red dust
  Of empires passed away;
The blood has turned their stones to rust,
  Their glory to decay.

And is it pride? Ah, that bright crown
  Has seemed to nations sweet;
But God has struck its luster down
  In ashes at His feet.

Not gold but only men can make
  A people great and strong;
Men who for truth and honor's sake
  Stand fast and suffer long.

Brave men who work while others sleep,
  Who dare while others fly . . .
They build a nation's pillars deep
  And lift them to the sky.

This Land and Flag

Author Unknown

What is the love of country for which our flag stands? Maybe it begins with love of the land itself. It is the fog rolling in with the tide at Eastport, or through the Golden Gate and among the towers of San Francisco. It is the sun coming up behind the White Mountains, over the Green, throwing a shining glory on Lake Champlain and above the Adirondacks. It is the storied Mississippi rolling swift and muddy past St. Louis, rolling past Cairo, pouring down past the levees of New Orleans. It is lazy noontide in the pines of Carolina; it is a sea of wheat rippling in western Kansas; it is the San Francisco peaks far north across the glowing nakedness of Arizona; it is the Grand Canyon, and a little stream coming down out of a New England ridge, in which are trout.

It is men at work. It is the storm-tossed fishermen coming into Gloucester and Provincetown and Astoria. It is the farmer riding his great machine in the dust of harvest, the dairyman going to the barn before sunrise; the lineman mending the broken wire; the miner drilling for the blast. It is the servants of fire in the murky splendor of Pittsburgh, between the Allegheny and the Monongahela; the trucks rumbling through the night, the locomotive engineer bringing the train in on time; the pilot in the clouds, the riveter running along the beam a hundred feet in air. It is the clerk in the office, the housewife doing the dishes and sending the children off to school. It is the teacher, doctor, and parson tending and helping, body and soul, for small reward.

It is stories told. It is the Pilgrims dying in their first dreadful winter. It is the minuteman standing his ground at Concord Bridge, and dying there. It is the army in rags, sick, freezing, starving at Valley Forge. It is the wagons and the men on foot going westward over Cumberland Gap, floating down the great rivers, rolling over the great plains. It is the settler hacking fiercely at the primeval forest on his new, his own lands. It is Thoreau at Walden Pond, Lincoln at Cooper Union, and Lee riding home from Appomattox. It is corruption and disgrace, answered always by men who would not let the flag lie in the dust, who have stood up in every generation to fight for the old ideals and the old rights, at risk of ruin or of life itself.

It is a great multitude of people on pilgrimage, common and ordinary people, charged with the usual human failings, yet filled with such a hope as never caught the imaginations and the hearts of any nation on earth before. The hope of liberty. The hope of justice. The hope of a land in which a man can stand straight, without fear, without rancor.

The land and the people and the flag . . . the land a continent, the people of every race, the flag a symbol of what humanity may aspire to when the wars are over and the barriers are down; to these each generation must be dedicated and consecrated anew, to defend with life itself, if need be, but above all, in friendliness, in hope, in courage, to live for.

The Spirit of America

Angelo Patri

Ahead are the children of the next generation. We are to carry to them the spirit of America. We must show them what went before, what lies ahead. We must lead them to seek, through the dimness of centuries, a gleaming line of silver white. It is the line of the Crusaders, steady, straight and strong, the quest for the Holy Grail, the search for freedom.

Back there, glimmering faintly in the dawn of history, stand the gods, their very names lost in the long ago.

There are the prophets, and the teachers, and the lawgivers, a mighty host.

There is Moses and those who followed him out of bondage.

There are the martyrs.

Now the line brightens and broadens. We are nearer. We can see some of the faces. These are Columbus, Washington, Lafayette, Garibaldi.

There is Lincoln.

There is Roosevelt.

There are the countless hosts who fought on the world's battlefields. We know them well.

The light streams from their faces. Their helmets gleam. Their swords flash fire. A fearless, dauntless, invincible army, they march on and on and on to the fullness of freedom. They live.

They are with us, children of America. They urge us on. They command us to go forward.

Man has slaved through the ages that we might be free. He has battled that we might have peace. He has studied that we might know. He has left us the heritage of the ages that we in our turn might carry it on.

Ahead of us are the children of the next generation. It is for them that we must live. It is for them that we must go on.

We are the torchbearers of liberty. We, too, must take our place in the search for freedom, the quest for the Holy Grail.

It is for this, we, the children of America, were born.

©

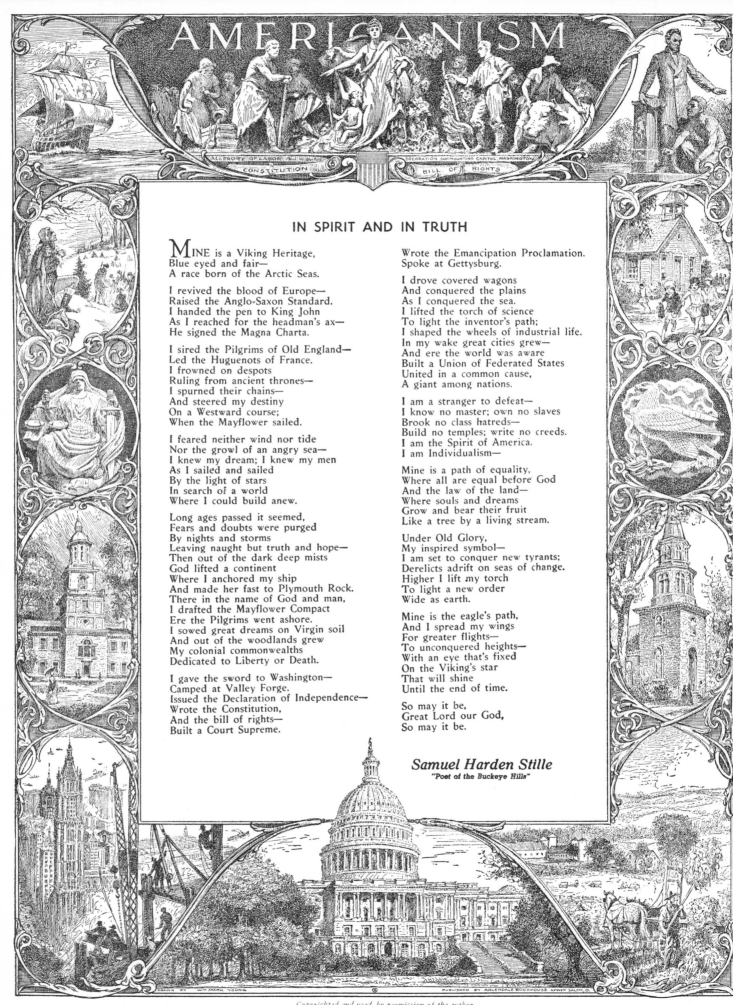

AMERICANISM

ALLEGORY OF LABOR
CONSTITUTION
DECORATION SURMOUNTING CAPITOL, WASHINGTON
BILL OF RIGHTS

IN SPIRIT AND IN TRUTH

Mine is a Viking Heritage,
Blue eyed and fair—
A race born of the Arctic Seas.

I revived the blood of Europe—
Raised the Anglo-Saxon Standard.
I handed the pen to King John
As I reached for the headman's ax—
He signed the Magna Charta.

I sired the Pilgrims of Old England—
Led the Huguenots of France.
I frowned on despots
Ruling from ancient thrones—
I spurned their chains—
And steered my destiny
On a Westward course;
When the Mayflower sailed.

I feared neither wind nor tide
Nor the growl of an angry sea—
I knew my dream; I knew my men
As I sailed and sailed
By the light of stars
In search of a world
Where I could build anew.

Long ages passed it seemed,
Fears and doubts were purged
By nights and storms
Leaving naught but truth and hope—
Then out of the dark deep mists
God lifted a continent
Where I anchored my ship
And made her fast to Plymouth Rock.
There in the name of God and man,
I drafted the Mayflower Compact
Ere the Pilgrims went ashore.
I sowed great dreams on Virgin soil
And out of the woodlands grew
My colonial commonwealths
Dedicated to Liberty or Death.

I gave the sword to Washington—
Camped at Valley Forge.
Issued the Declaration of Independence—
Wrote the Constitution,
And the bill of rights—
Built a Court Supreme.

Wrote the Emancipation Proclamation.
Spoke at Gettysburg.

I drove covered wagons
And conquered the plains
As I conquered the sea.
I lifted the torch of science
To light the inventor's path;
I shaped the wheels of industrial life.
In my wake great cities grew—
And ere the world was aware
Built a Union of Federated States
United in a common cause,
A giant among nations.

I am a stranger to defeat—
I know no master; own no slaves
Brook no class hatreds—
Build no temples; write no creeds.
I am the Spirit of America.
I am Individualism—

Mine is a path of equality,
Where all are equal before God
And the law of the land—
Where souls and dreams
Grow and bear their fruit
Like a tree by a living stream.

Under Old Glory,
My inspired symbol—
I am set to conquer new tyrants;
Derelicts adrift on seas of change.
Higher I lift my torch
To light a new order
Wide as earth.

Mine is the eagle's path,
And I spread my wings
For greater flights—
To unconquered heights—
With an eye that's fixed
On the Viking's star
That will shine
Until the end of time.

So may it be,
Great Lord our God,
So may it be.

Samuel Harden Stille
"Poet of the Buckeye Hills"

DRAWN BY WM. MARK YOUNG
PUBLISHED BY ARLENDALE BOOKHOUSE, LOWER SALEM, O.

The God who gave us LIFE, gave us LIBERTY at the same time.

Th Jefferson

PAUL MANN

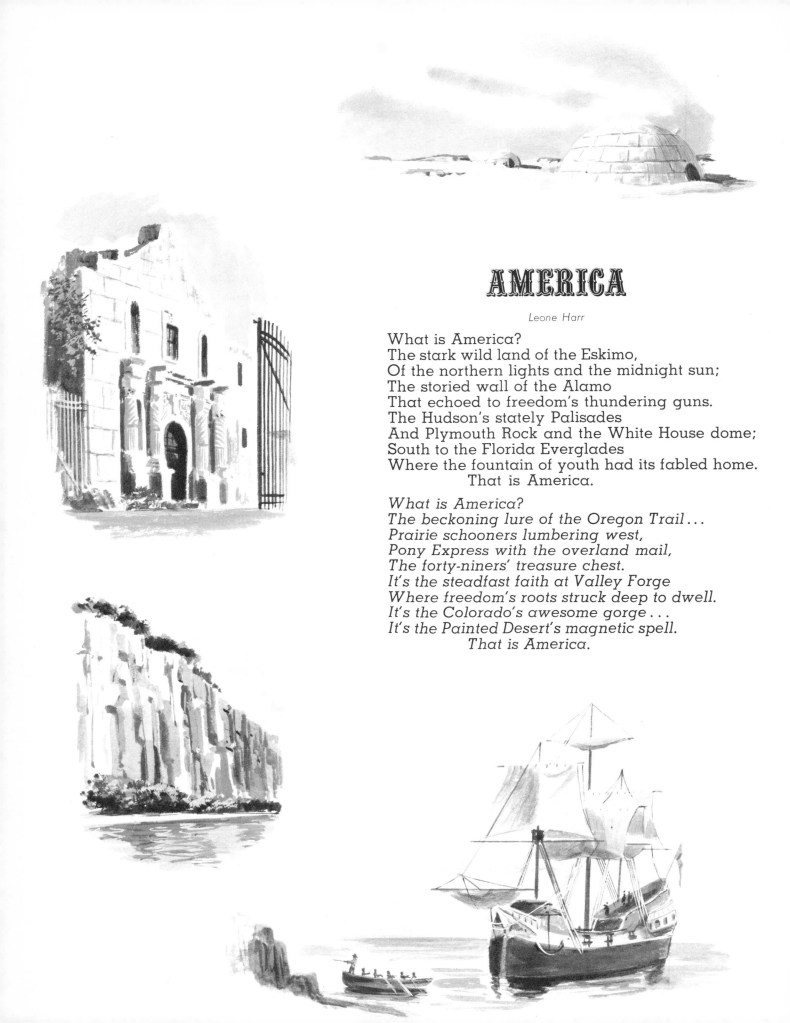

AMERICA

Leone Harr

What is America?
The stark wild land of the Eskimo,
Of the northern lights and the midnight sun;
The storied wall of the Alamo
That echoed to freedom's thundering guns.
The Hudson's stately Palisades
And Plymouth Rock and the White House dome;
South to the Florida Everglades
Where the fountain of youth had its fabled home.
That is America.

What is America?
The beckoning lure of the Oregon Trail...
Prairie schooners lumbering west,
Pony Express with the overland mail,
The forty-niners' treasure chest.
It's the steadfast faith at Valley Forge
Where freedom's roots struck deep to dwell.
It's the Colorado's awesome gorge...
It's the Painted Desert's magnetic spell.
That is America.

What is America?
It's the city known as the melting pot
Where Liberty's torch is held on high.
It's the Unknown Soldier's burial plot;
It's the evening star in the sunset sky.
It's the age-old calm of the towering peaks;
It's the scent of sage in the rain-swept air.
It's the call of the wilderness that speaks
To the venturesome few who its dangers dare.
                    That is America.

What is America?
It's the reaching spire of the village church
That bears aloft our prayers to God.
It's the eagle's scream from his lofty perch;
It's the life that springs from the lowly sod.
It's your land and my land held in trust
For those who died on land and sea;
Keep it the same for them we must
In all its glorious traditions . . . for we
                    Are Americans.

©

Patriotism

Sir Walter Scott

Breathes there the man with soul so dead,
Who never to himself hath said,
"This is my own, my native land!"
Whose heart hath ne'er within him burned
As home his footsteps he hath turned
From wandering on a foreign strand?
If such there breathe, go, mark him well;
For him no minstrel raptures swell;
High though his titles, proud his name,
Boundless his wealth as wish can claim;
Despite those titles, power, and pelf,
The wretch, concentred all in self,
Living, shall forfeit fair renown,
And, doubly dying, shall go down
To the vile dust from whence he sprung,
Unwept, unhonored and unsung.

LIBERTY BELL

Bessie Price Owen

The East where liberty was born,
Where soldiers fought and fell,
In seventeen seventy-six
Rang the Liberty Bell.
The East that gave to us the creed
To honor God and the right
To love the flag that o'er us waves,
To keep it pure and white.

The West where deserts hot with sand
Raise gardens, new and fair,
Where mountain peaks reach to the sky,
And God is everywhere.
The East that gave to us new light
So man could catch the ray
And make of it a paradise
Where travelers rest and stay.

The North where winds so cold and strong
Sweep through the plains and fields,
And men that toil with steel and soil
A mighty power wield.
The North that gave to us new strength,
The Union, liberty . . .
And Lincoln's heritage of truth
For all posterity.

The South where balmy breezes blow,
Where sparkling brooks flow by,
Where life is simple and sincere,
Where faith can never die.
The South that gave to us ideals
That throb along the way . . .
General Robert E. Lee's surrender
On a history-making day.

The East and West, the North and South,
A blend of love and pride,
A heritage so precious
That always will abide.
Our glorious America
Sprang from the simple sod
Where man dreamed, toiled and conquered . . .
"One nation under God."

©

AMERICA

Edgar Daniel Kramer

Ring out once more across the world
Of harsh and futile strife;
Ring out and fill our hearts with dreams
That are the breath of life.
Ring out and make us see again
The brightly gleaming star
That we have lost amid the gloom,
As we have wandered far
From ways wherein our fathers fared
To find their shining goals,
For we are groping through the dark
With anxiety in our souls.

Ring out across the hills and plains,
Ring out across the seas,
Ring out and make us know again
The old simplicities
That gave our sturdy fathers strength
To make their dreams come true,
As they shaped in the wilderness
A nation nobly new.
Ring out and lead our stumbling feet
From ways where gray ghosts nod
To paths our fathers humbly walked
With faith in man and God.

©

Let's Ring the Bells

Sara Mansfield

Let's ring the bells for freedom . . .
Oh, let's ring them loud and clear!
Let's let the world around us know
We hold our freedom dear!

Of course we have our problems,
But we've solved them other times.
We will again! And fairly!
So ring out the freedom chimes!

We're not Utopia, we know,
But here a man has worth,
And here his dreams can count for more
Than elsewhere on the earth.

Beloved land! We're proud of you!
We lift your banner high,
And send the bells for freedom
Pealing out across the sky!

But let them also ring for peace,
And give them triple worth
By letting freedom's hopes ring out
For every man on earth.

©

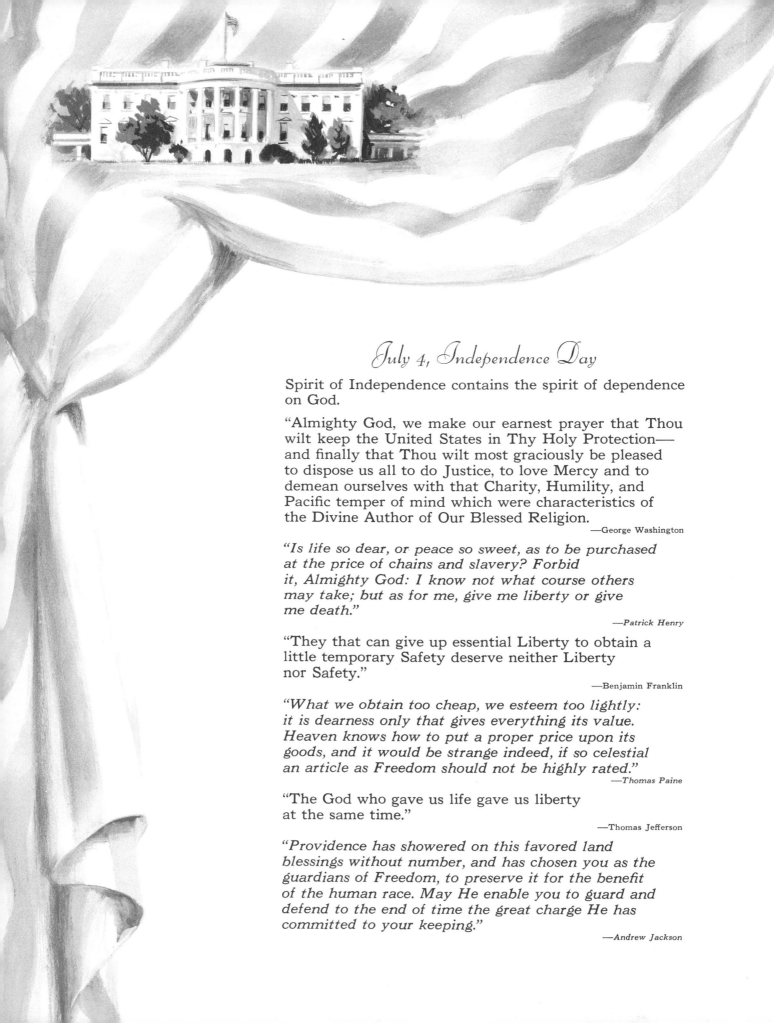

July 4, Independence Day

Spirit of Independence contains the spirit of dependence on God.

"Almighty God, we make our earnest prayer that Thou wilt keep the United States in Thy Holy Protection— and finally that Thou wilt most graciously be pleased to dispose us all to do Justice, to love Mercy and to demean ourselves with that Charity, Humility, and Pacific temper of mind which were characteristics of the Divine Author of Our Blessed Religion.

—George Washington

"Is life so dear, or peace so sweet, as to be purchased at the price of chains and slavery? Forbid it, Almighty God: I know not what course others may take; but as for me, give me liberty or give me death."

—*Patrick Henry*

"They that can give up essential Liberty to obtain a little temporary Safety deserve neither Liberty nor Safety."

—Benjamin Franklin

"What we obtain too cheap, we esteem too lightly: it is dearness only that gives everything its value. Heaven knows how to put a proper price upon its goods, and it would be strange indeed, if so celestial an article as Freedom should not be highly rated."

—*Thomas Paine*

"The God who gave us life gave us liberty at the same time."

—Thomas Jefferson

"Providence has showered on this favored land blessings without number, and has chosen you as the guardians of Freedom, to preserve it for the benefit of the human race. May He enable you to guard and defend to the end of time the great charge He has committed to your keeping."

—*Andrew Jackson*

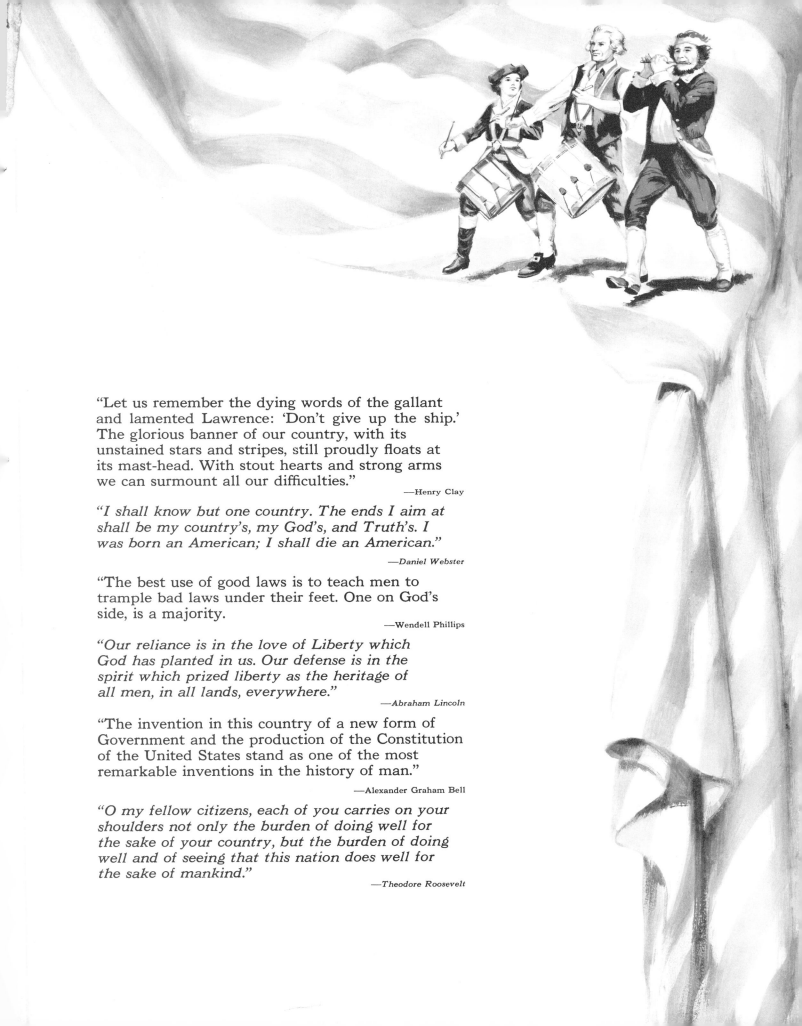

"Let us remember the dying words of the gallant and lamented Lawrence: 'Don't give up the ship.' The glorious banner of our country, with its unstained stars and stripes, still proudly floats at its mast-head. With stout hearts and strong arms we can surmount all our difficulties."

—Henry Clay

"I shall know but one country. The ends I aim at shall be my country's, my God's, and Truth's. I was born an American; I shall die an American."

—*Daniel Webster*

"The best use of good laws is to teach men to trample bad laws under their feet. One on God's side, is a majority.

—Wendell Phillips

"Our reliance is in the love of Liberty which God has planted in us. Our defense is in the spirit which prized liberty as the heritage of all men, in all lands, everywhere."

—*Abraham Lincoln*

"The invention in this country of a new form of Government and the production of the Constitution of the United States stand as one of the most remarkable inventions in the history of man."

—Alexander Graham Bell

"O my fellow citizens, each of you carries on your shoulders not only the burden of doing well for the sake of your country, but the burden of doing well and of seeing that this nation does well for the sake of mankind."

—*Theodore Roosevelt*

When, in the Course of human events, it becomes necessary for one people to dissolve the political bands which have connected them with another, and to assume, among the Powers of the earth, the separate and equal station to which the Laws of Nature and of Nature's God entitle them, a decent respect to the opinions of mankind requires that they should declare the causes which impel them to the separation.

We hold these truths to be self-evident: that all men are created equal; that they are endowed by their Creator with certain unalienable Rights; that among these are Life, Liberty, and the Pursuit of Happiness. That, to secure these Rights, Governments are instituted among Men, deriving their just powers from the consent of the governed. That, whenever any Form of Government becomes destructive of these ends, it is the Right of the People to alter or to abolish it, and to institute new Government, laying its foundation on such Principles, and organizing its Powers in such form, as to them shall seem most likely to effect their Safety and Happiness. Prudence, indeed, will dictate that Governments long established should not be changed for light and transient causes; and, accordingly, all experience hath shewn that mankind are more disposed to suffer, while evils are sufferable, than to right themselves by abolishing the forms to which they are accustomed. But, when a long train of abuses and usurpations, pursuing invariably the same Object, evinces a design to reduce them under absolute Despotism, it is their right, it is their duty, to throw off such Government, and to provide new Guards for their security. Such has been the patient sufferance of these Colonies, and such is now the necessity which constrains them to alter their former Systems of Government.

We, therefore, the representatives of the United States of America, in General Congress Assembled, appealing to the Supreme Judge of the world for the rectitude of our intentions, do, in the name and by the Authority of the good people of these Colonies, solemnly publish and declare that these United Colonies are, and of Right ought to be, Free and Independent States; that they are absolved from all Allegiance to the British Crown, and that all political connection between them and the State of Great Britain is, and ought to be, totally dissolved; and that, as Free and Independent States, they have full Power to levy War, conclude Peace, contract Alliances, establish Commerce, and to do all other Acts and Things which Independent States may of right do. And, for the support of this Declaration, with a firm reliance on the Protection of Divine Providence, we mutually pledge to each other our Lives, our Fortunes, and our sacred Honor.

from The Declaration Of Independence
July 4, 1776.

Give Us Men!

Josiah Gilbert Holland

Give us Men!
Men—from every rank,
Fresh and free and frank;
Men of thought and reading,
Men of light and leading,
Men of loyal breeding,
The nation's welfare speeding;
Men of faith and not of fiction,
Men of lofty aim in action;
Give us Men—I say again,
Give us Men!

Give us Men!
Strong and stalwart ones;
Men whom highest hope inspires,
Men whom purest honor fires,
Men who trample self beneath them,
Men who make their country wreathe them
As her noble sons,
Worthy of their sires;
Men who never shame their mothers,
Men who never fail their brothers,
True, however false are others:
Give us Men—I say again,
Give us Men!

Give us Men!
Men who, when the tempest gathers,
Grasp the standard of their fathers
In the thickest fight;
Men who strike for home and altar,
(Let the coward cringe and falter),
God defend the right!
True as truth the lorn and lonely,
Tender, as the brave are only;
Men who tread where saints have trod,
Men for Country, Home—and God:
Give us Men! I say again—again—
Give us Men!

Abraham Lincoln is one of America's immortals. He grows in the affections of the people with each passing year. He was a product of our civilization, reared among the people, and their friend. He has seldom, if ever, been surpassed in simplicity of expression and force of argument. He was wholly devoted to his country's welfare and followed lofty ideals. He fought principles rather than men, and thus avoided the bitterness of personal antagonisms. His birth, his boyhood, his political contests, his public life and his tragical death combined to give him a unique place in our nation's history.

William Jennings Bryan

To know him personally was to love and respect him for his great qualities of heart and head, and for his patience and patriotism. With all his disappointments from failures on the part of those to whom he had entrusted command, and treachery on the part of those who had gained his confidence but to betray it, I never heard him utter a complaint, nor cast a censure for bad conduct or bad faith. It was his nature to find excuses for his adversaries. A man of great ability, pure patriotism, unselfish nature, full of forgiveness to his enemies, bearing malice toward none, he proved to be the man above all others for the great struggle through which the nation had to pass to place itself among the greatest in the family of nations. In his death the nation lost its greatest hero, in his death the South lost its most just friend.

Ulysses S. Grant

Paul Revere's Ride

Henry Wadsworth Longfellow

Listen, my children, and you shall hear
Of the midnight ride of Paul Revere,
On the eighteenth of April, in seventy-five;
Hardly a man is now alive
Who remembers that famous day and year.

*He said to his friend, "If the British march
By land or sea from the town tonight,
Hang a lantern aloft in the belfry arch
Of the North Church tower as a signal light:
One, if by land, and two, if by sea,
And I on the opposite shore will be
Ready to ride and spread the alarm
Through every Middlesex village and farm,
For the country folk to be up and to arm."*

Then he said, "Good-night!" and with muffled oar
Silently rowed to the Charlestown shore
Just as the moon rose over the bay
Where swinging wide at her moorings lay
The Somerset, British man-of-war;
A phantom ship, with each mast and spar
Across the moon like a prison bar,
And a huge black hulk that was magnified
By its own reflection in the tide.

*Meanwhile, his friend, through alley and street,
Wanders and watches with eager ears
Till in the silence around him he hears
The muster of men at the barrack door,
The sound of arms and the tramp of feet,
And the measured tread of the grenadiers
Marching down to their boats on the shore.*

Then he climbed the tower of the Old North Church,
By the wooden stairs, with stealthy tread,
To the belfry-chamber overhead
And startled the pigeons from their perch
On the somber rafters that round him made
Masses and moving shapes of shade . . .
By the trembling ladder, steep and tall,
To the highest window in the wall
Where he paused to listen and look down
A moment on the roofs of the town,
And the moonlight flowing over all.

Beneath, in the churchyard lay the dead
In their night encampment on the hill,
Wrapped in silence so deep and still
That he could hear, like a sentinel's tread,
The watchful night-wind as it went
Creeping along from tent to tent,
And seeming to whisper, "All is well!"
A moment only he feels the spell
Of the place and the hour and the secret dread
Of the lonely belfry and the dead:
For suddenly all his thoughts are bent
On a shadowy something far away
Where the river widens to meet the bay,
A line of black that bends and floats
On the rising tide like a bridge of boats.

Meanwhile, impatient to mount and ride,
Booted and spurred, with a heavy stride
On the opposite shore walked Paul Revere.
Now he patted his horse's side,
Now gazed at the landscape far and near;
Then, impetuous, stamped the earth,
And turned and tightened his saddle-girth;
But mostly he watched with eager search
The belfry-tower of the Old North Church
As it rose above the graves on the hill,
Lonely and spectral and somber and still.
And lo! as he looks, on the belfry's height
A glimmer, and then a gleam of light!
He springs to the saddle, the bridle he turns
But lingers and gazes till full on his sight
A second lamp in the belfry burns.

A hurry of hoofs in a village street,
A shape in the moonlight, a bulk in the dark,
And beneath, from the pebbles, in passing, a spark
Struck out by a steed flying fearless and fleet.
That was all! And yet, through the gloom and the light
The fate of a nation was riding that night:
And the spark struck out by that steed in his flight
Kindled the land into flame with its heat.

He has left the village and mounted the steep,
And beneath him, tranquil and broad and deep,
Is the Mystic, meeting the ocean tides;
And under the alders that skirt its edge,
Now soft on the sand, now loud on the ledge,
Is heard the tramp of his steed as he rides.

It was twelve by the village clock
When he crossed the bridge into Medford town.
He heard the crowing of the cock
And the barking of the farmer's dog,
And felt the damp of the river fog
That rises after the sun goes down.

It was one by the village clock
When he galloped into Lexington.
He saw the gilded weathercock
Swim in the moonlight as he passed,
And the meeting-house windows, blank and bare,
Gaze at him with a spectral glare
As if they already stood aghast
At the bloody work they would look upon.

It was two by the village clock
When he came to the bridge in Concord town.
He heard the bleating of the flock
And the twitter of birds among the trees,
And felt the breath of the morning breeze
Blowing over the meadows brown.
And one was safe and asleep in his bed
Who at the bridge would be first to fall,
Who that day would be lying dead,
Pierced by a British musket-ball.

You know the rest. In the books you have read
How the British Regulars fired and fled,
How the farmers gave them ball for ball
From behind each fence and farmyard wall,
Chasing the redcoats down the lane . . .
Then crossing the fields to emerge again
Under the trees at the turn of the road,
And only pausing to fire and load.
So through the night went his cry of alarm
To every Middlesex village and farm,
A cry of defiance and not of fear,
A voice in the darkness, a knock at the door,
And a word that shall echo forevermore!
For, borne on the night-wind of the past,
Through all our history, to the last,
In the hour of darkness and peril and need,
The people will waken and listen to hear
The hurrying hoofbeats of that steed
And the midnight message of Paul Revere.

MAXIMS

FROM

POOR RICHARD

A good example is the best sermon.

*A long life may not be good enough, but a good life is
long enough.*

Better is little with content than too much with contention.

*Great beauty, great strength, and great riches are really
and truly of no great use; a right heart exceeds all.*

Who pleasure gives, shall joy receive.

*Content makes poor men rich; discontent makes rich
men poor.*

Lost time is never found again.

Keep thy shop, and thy shop will keep thee.

Little strokes fell great oaks.

Who is rich? He that rejoices in his portion.

Wink at small faults—remember thou hast great ones.

Search others for their virtues, thyself for thy vices.

Anger is never without a reason, but seldom with a good one.

*Fools need advice most, but wise men only are the better
for it.*

He that falls in love with himself will have no rivals.

*Neglect mending a small fault, and 'twill soon be a
great one.*

The doors of wisdom are never shut.

*For want of a nail the shoe is lost; for want of a shoe
the horse is lost; for want of a horse the rider is lost.*

Better slip with foot than tongue.

God helps them that help themselves.

Never leave that to tomorrow which you can do today.

He that goes a-borrowing goes a-sorrowing.

It is hard for an empty sack to stand upright.

He that riseth late must trot all day.

Making a Nation Great

Alexander Blackburn

Not serried ranks with flags unfurled,
Not armored ships that gird the world,
Not hoarded wealth or busy mills,
Not cattle on a thousand hills;

Not sages wise, or schools, or laws,
Not boasted deeds in freedom's cause . . .
All these may be and yet the state
In eye of God be far from great.

That land is great which knows the Lord,
Whose sons are guided by His word,
Where justice rules twixt man and man,
Where love controls in act and plan.

Where breathing in his native air
Each soul finds joy in praise and prayer . . .
Thus may our country, good and great,
Be God's delight—man's best estate.

*Our sincere thanks to the author
whose address we were unable to locate.*

Abraham Lincoln

Bessie Price Owen

Almost a century but never a day
 Goes by without some sign
Of living tribute and respect
 To his immortal shrine.

He belongs to every creed and class,
 To every human race . . .
This great but simple quiet man
 With sorrow in his face.

Those tired sunken kindly eyes,
 They look compassionately
And stir our very being
 With divine tranquility.

Short-lived his noble dream we know
 To unite this wondrous land
Into one great mighty nation . . .
 The Union strong and grand.

But though his work was ended
 And a nation broken lay,
His truth goes marching on and on
 Into eternal day.

And down through history's pages
 His name will hallowed be
For preserving this great nation
 For all posterity.

©

THE OATH OF A FREE-MAN

I (*A.B.*) being by Gods providence, an Inhabitant, and Freeman, within the Jurisdiction of this Commonwealth; do freely acknowledge my self to be subject to the Government thereof: And therefore do here swear by the great and dreadful Name of the Ever-living God, that *I* will be true and faithfull to the same, and will accordingly yield assistance & support thereunto, with my person and estate, as in equity *I* am bound; and will also truly endeavour to maintain and preserve all the liberties and priviledges thereof, submitting my self to the wholesome Lawes & Orders made and established by the same.

And further, that *I* will not plot or practice any evill against it, or consent to any that shall so do; but will timely discover and reveal the same to lawfull Authority now here established, for the speedy preventing thereof. ¶ Moreover, *I* doe solemnly bind my self in the sight of God, that when *I* shal be called to give my voyce touching any such matter of this State, in which Freemen are to deal, *I* will give my vote and suffrage as *I* shall judge in mine own conscience may best conduce and tend to the publike weal of the body, without respect of persons, or favour of any man. So help me God in the Lord Jesus Christ.

This Oath of a Free-Man was the first printed piece produced in Colonial America by Stephen Daye

Political Religion of America

Abraham Lincoln

Let every American, every lover of liberty, every well-wisher to his posterity, swear by the blood of the Revolution, never to violate in the least particular, the laws of the country, and never tolerate their violation by others. As the patriots of '76 did to the support of the Declaration of Independence, so to the support of the Constitution and laws let every American pledge his life, his property and his sacred honor. Let every man remember that to violate the law is to trample on the blood of his father, and to tear the charter of his own and his children's liberty.

Let reverence for the laws be breathed by every American mother to the lisping babe that prattles on her lap. Let it be taught in the schools, in seminaries and in colleges. Let it be written in primers, spelling-books and in almanacs. Let it be preached from the pulpit, proclaimed in legislative halls, and enforced in courts of justice; and in short, let it become the political religion of the nation. And let the old and the young, the rich and the poor, the grave and the gay of all sexes and tongues and colors and conditions, sacrifice unceasingly upon its altars.

Peace Will Come

Garnett Ann Schultz

Peace will come on a brighter day
When a fairer dawn shall break,
And the guns of war shall be laid aside
With the toll of lives they take.
Stars will shine in a peaceful sky
Where clouds shall be no more,
And every smile will bring happiness
Without a thought of war.

Peace will rule in a fearless world
Where right shall surely win,
And eyes will glow with a sweet content
Where doubts and tears have been.
Where once a kiss brought a longing ache
For the loved one far away,
And only a mem'ry filled the heart
Where a dear one couldn't stay.

Peace will come . . . we must never doubt,
For faith must last through all,
Though precious boys must pay the price
And heed their country's call.
We must be as sure of our victory,
For true as the setting sun,
We'll never lose if we keep the thought
That some day peace will come.

©

Famous Men

Arthur Guiterman

Forever honor those who, great of heart,
Reared up the land we love and made it strong!
God give us equal strength to do our part
As they did theirs, like them to face all wrong
Unflinchingly. As they were brave and just,
So may we prove; and yet, as time in flight
Brings other ways and better ways we trust,
May we find nobler means to aid the right
Than their day knew. God's road is all uphill
And man climbs slowly. These were fine and true,
But we must bear their banner higher still;
What else would those we honor have us do?
The past's a scroll whereon great truths are found,
But not a chain by which men's feet are bound.

Lincoln

Homer Hock

There is no new thing to be said of
Lincoln. There is no new thing to be
said of mountains, or of the sea, or
of the stars. The years may go their
way, but the same old mountains lift
their granite shoulders above the
drifting clouds, the same mysterious
seas beat upon the shore, and the
same silent stars keep holy vigil above
a tired world. But to mountains and
seas and stars men turn forever in
unwearied homage. And thus with
Lincoln. For he was mountain in
grandeur of soul; he was sea in deep
under-voice of mystic loneliness; he
was star in steadfast purity of purpose and of service. And he abides.

*Our sincere thanks to the author
whose address we were unable to locate*

THE AMERICAN'S CREED

"Breathes there a man with soul so dead, who never to himself hath said, this is my own, my native land."

SCOTT

I believe in the United States of America, as a government of the people, by the people, for the people; whose just powers are derived from the consent of the governed; a democracy in a republic; a sovereign nation of many sovereign states; a perfect union, one and inseparable; established upon those principles of freedom, equality, justice and humanity for which American patriots sacrificed their lives and fortunes.

I therefore believe it is my duty to my country to love it, to support its constitution, to obey its laws, to respect its flag, and to defend it against all enemies.

The American's Creed by William Tyler Page was adopted by an Act of Congress, April 6, 1918.

There is no place in civilization for the idler. None of us has any right to ease.

Henry Ford

God grants lib-
erty to those who
love it, and are
always ready to
guard and defend
it.

Daniel Webster

Few men durin[g]
their lifetim[e]
come anywhe[re]
near exhaustin[g]
the resource[s]
dwelling with[in]
them. There a[re]
deep wells [of]
strength that a[re]
never used.

Admiral Richard By[rd]

Everything
comes to him who
hustles while he
waits.

Thomas A. Edison

Where we love
is home...home
that our feet may
leave, but not our
hearts.

Oliver Wendell Holmes

I wish to preach,
not the doctrine
of ignoble ease,
but the doctrine
of the strenuous
life.

Theodore Roosevelt

Grief can take care of itself, but to get the full value of a joy you must have somebody to divide it with.

Mark Twain

Knowledge comes, but wisdom lingers.

Alfred Lord Tennyson

Lives of great men all remind us we can make our lives sublime, and departing, leave behind us footprints on the sands of time.

Henry Wadsworth Longfellow

Associate with men of good quality if you esteem your own reputation; for it is better to be alone than in bad company.

George Washington

The most beautiful thing we can experience is the mysterious. It is the source of all true art and science.

Albert Einstein

If we had paid no more attention to our plants than we have to our children, we would now be living in a jungle of weeds.

Luther Burbank

Ask not what your country can do for you; Ask what you can do for your country

John F. Kennedy

PAUL MANN

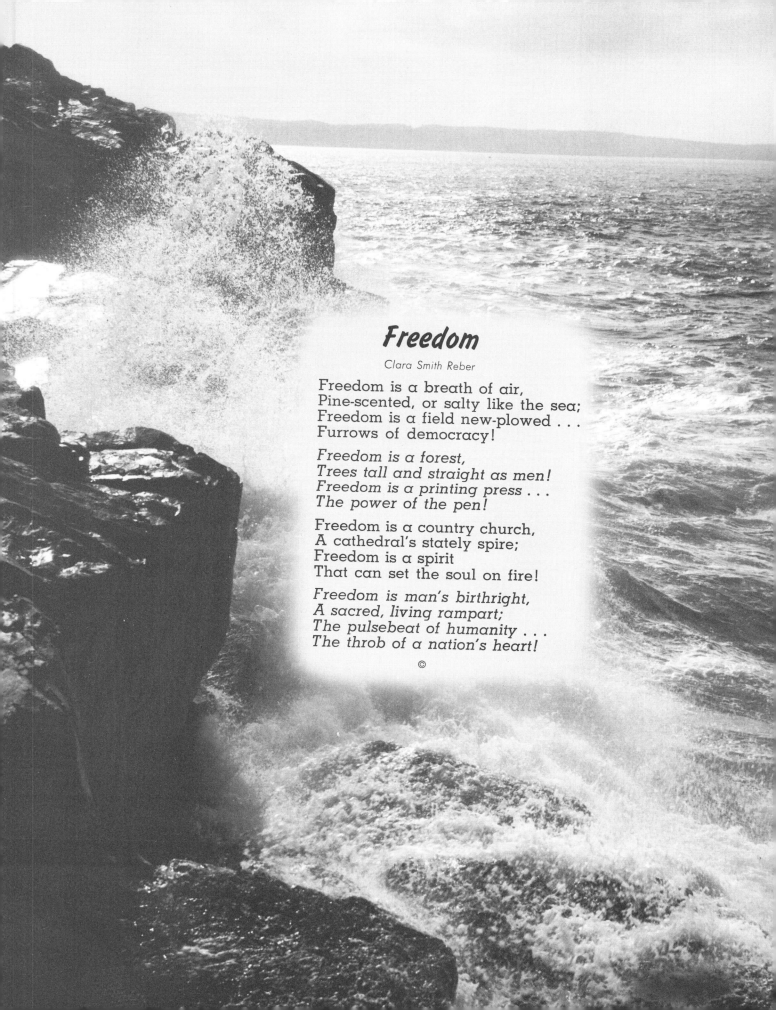

Freedom

Clara Smith Reber

Freedom is a breath of air,
Pine-scented, or salty like the sea;
Freedom is a field new-plowed . . .
Furrows of democracy!

Freedom is a forest,
Trees tall and straight as men!
Freedom is a printing press . . .
The power of the pen!

Freedom is a country church,
A cathedral's stately spire;
Freedom is a spirit
That can set the soul on fire!

Freedom is man's birthright,
A sacred, living rampart;
The pulsebeat of humanity . . .
The throb of a nation's heart!

©

Old Glory

Harold A. Schulz

I thrill to watch Old Glory fly
And wave her gleaming colors high.
Therein the red, the white and blue . . .
I see a nation great and true;
A country made of men who dared
To fight and die because they cared,
Who, yet today, defend each right
To keep aflame our freedom's light.

Free speech, free press, free enterprise
Are banners waving in the skies;
The right to live, the right to pray
And worship God in one's own way . . .
These are the truths unvarying
For which men bleed and work and sing.
What noble task is there for me
To help preserve our liberty?
Instead of malice, greed and hate,
These freedoms I must demonstrate.

Our nation, founded under God,
Must share its good across earth's sod,
For only then will all men know
What loyal seed their lives may grow.
I see in this kaleidoscope
Our sacred trust, our every hope.
Blest symbol of the free and brave,
I thrill to watch Old Glory wave.

©

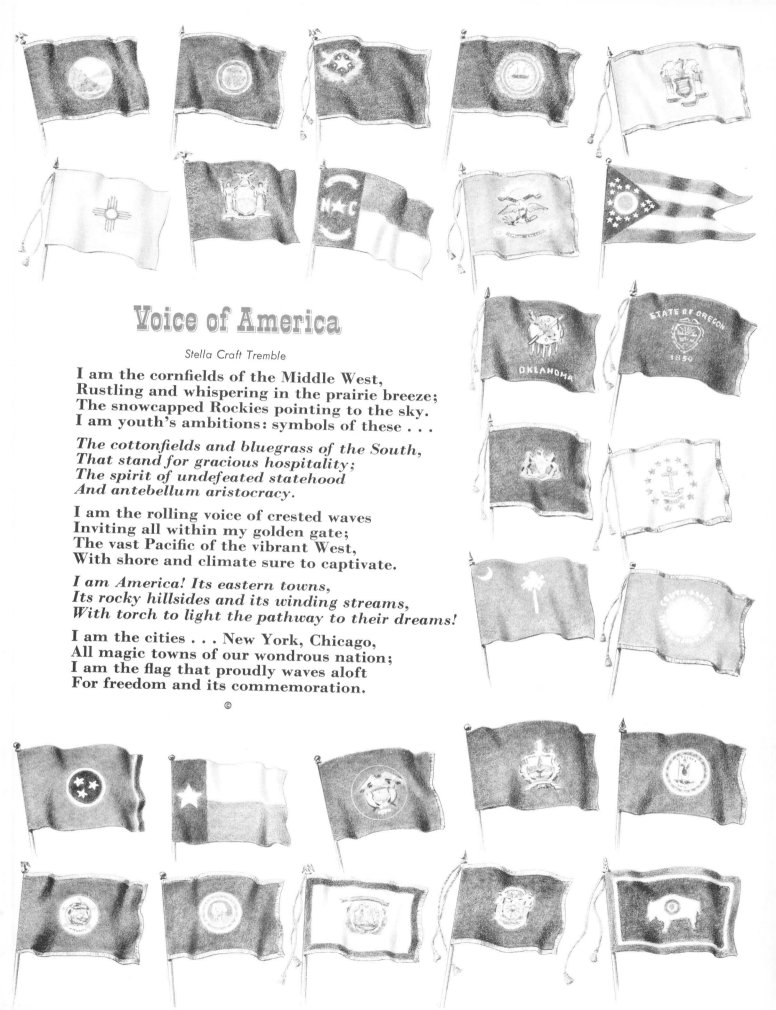

Voice of America

Stella Craft Tremble

I am the cornfields of the Middle West,
Rustling and whispering in the prairie breeze;
The snowcapped Rockies pointing to the sky.
I am youth's ambitions: symbols of these . . .

The cottonfields and bluegrass of the South,
That stand for gracious hospitality;
The spirit of undefeated statehood
And antebellum aristocracy.

I am the rolling voice of crested waves
Inviting all within my golden gate;
The vast Pacific of the vibrant West,
With shore and climate sure to captivate.

I am America! Its eastern towns,
Its rocky hillsides and its winding streams,
With torch to light the pathway to their dreams!

I am the cities . . . New York, Chicago,
All magic towns of our wondrous nation;
I am the flag that proudly waves aloft
For freedom and its commemoration.

©

A Memory

Emma A. Lent

A day of tender memory,
A day of sacred hours,
Of little bands of marching men,
Of drums and flags and flowers.

A day when a great nation halts
Its mighty throbbing pace,
And by its meed of gratitude
Shows love with willing grace.

A day to keep from year to year
In memory of the dead;
Let music sound and flowers be laid
Upon each resting bed.

Memorial Day

Edgar A. Guest

Blow gently, winds of May,
And softly stir the trees,
Whispering today
The love we bear to these
Who sleep that silent sleep,
At rest forevermore.
Blow gently, winds of May . . .
Their warfare now is o'er.

Blow gently, winds of May,
Bearing the perfume rare
Of blossoms o'er the way;
Rose petals scatter there;
The starry flag we place
In glory on each grave,
Catches in a fond embrace
For us and proudly waves.

Blow gently, winds of May,
Shine softly, summer sun;
Our heroes sleep today,
Their duty nobly done.
And with the flag they loved,
And flowers, we come today
To honor those who sleep . . .
Blow gently, winds of May.

DUTY ☆ HONOR ☆ COUNTRY

Duty—Honor—Country. Those three hallowed words reverently dictate what you ought to be, what you can be, what you will be. They are your rallying points: to build courage when courage seems to fail; to regain faith when there seems to be little cause for faith; to create hope when hope becomes forlorn. They build your basic character, they make you strong enough to know when you are weak, and brave enough to face yourself when you are afraid. They teach you to be proud and unbending in honest failure, but humble and gentle in success; not to substitute words for actions, nor to seek the path of comfort, but to face the stress and spur of difficulty and challenge; to learn to stand up in the storm but to have compassion on those who fall; to master yourself before you seek to master others; to have a heart that is clean, a goal that is high; to learn to laugh yet never forget how to weep; to reach into the future yet never neglect the past; to be serious yet never to take yourself too seriously; to be modest so that you will remember the simplicity of true greatness, the open mind of true wisdom, the meekness of true strength. They give you a temper of the will, a quality of the imagination, a vigor of the emotions, a freshness of the deep springs of life, a temperamental predominance of courage over timidity, an appetite for adventure over love of ease. They create in your heart the sense of wonder, the unfailing hope of what next, and the joy and inspiration of life.

Used by permission of Mrs. Douglas MacArthur   *General Douglas MacArthur*